Visit and Learn

Mesa Verde

by Kelsey Jopp

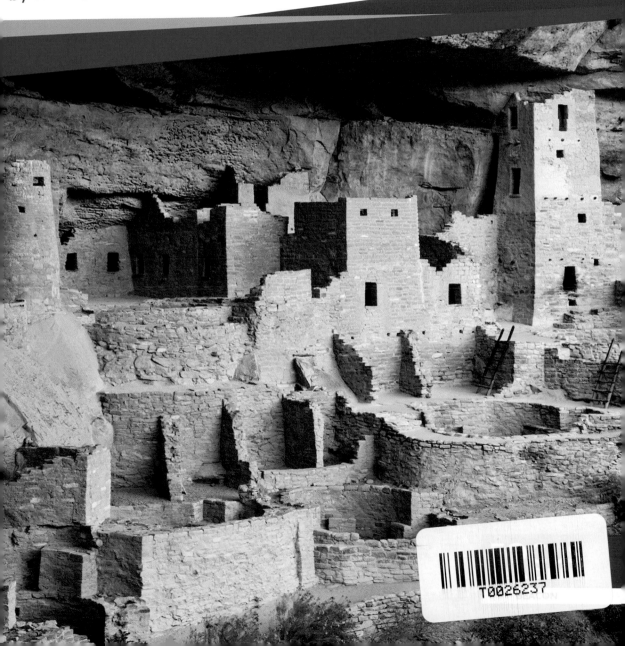

www.focusreaders.com

Focus Readers is distributed by North Star Editions:
sales@northstareditions.com | 888-417-0195

Produced for Focus Readers by Red Line Editorial.

Photographs ©: Shutterstock Images, cover, 1, 4, 7, 11, 13, 14, 17, 22, 25, 26, 29; Grand Canyon National Park Museum Collection/US National Park Service, 8; iStockphoto, 19, 20–21

Library of Congress Cataloging-in-Publication Data
Names: Jopp, Kelsey, 1993- author.
Title: Mesa Verde / by Kelsey Jopp.
Description: Lake Elmo, MN : Focus Readers, [2024] | Series: Visit and
  learn | Includes bibliographical references and index. | Audience:
  Grades 2-3
Identifiers: LCCN 2023008338 (print) | LCCN 2023008339 (ebook) | ISBN
  9781637396186 (hardcover) | ISBN 9781637396759 (paperback) | ISBN
  9781637397855 (ebook pdf) | ISBN 9781637397329 (hosted ebook)
Subjects: LCSH: Mesa Verde National Park (Colo.)--Juvenile literature.
Classification: LCC F782.M52 J67 2024 (print) | LCC F782.M52 (ebook) |
  DDC 978.8/27--dc23/eng/20230322
LC record available at https://lccn.loc.gov/2023008338
LC ebook record available at https://lccn.loc.gov/2023008339

Printed in the United States of America
Mankato, MN
082023

About the Author

Kelsey Jopp is an editor, writer, and lifelong learner. She lives in Minnesota, where she enjoys swimming in lakes and playing endless fetch with her sheltie, Teddy.

Table of Contents

Chapter 1

The Green Table

The sun sets over Mesa Verde. The dry air grows cool. An owl calls out. A wide, flat cliff stretches across the land. Stone buildings stand below. They glow in the orange light.

 The buildings at Mesa Verde face southwest. That way, they get more heat from the sun during winter.

Each building is different. Some are square and tall. Others are round and low. Together, they form a town. But no one lives there anymore. Only **ruins** remain.

In Spanish, *Mesa Verde* means "green table." The mesa is a flat mountain. Green trees grow on top. **Ancestral Puebloans** lived here

Did You Know?

The cliffs in Mesa Verde block the sun. This cooled the homes during summer.

 There are more than 600 homes at Mesa Verde.

hundreds of years ago. They built homes in the mesa's cliffs.

Today, Mesa Verde is a national park in Colorado. People visit from near and far.

Chapter 2

History in Stone

Around 550 CE, the Basketmakers arrived in Mesa Verde. They were ancestors of Ancestral Puebloans. The Basketmakers built pit houses on the mesa. These houses were dug 3 feet (1 m) underground.

 The Basketmakers made baskets out of plant fibers.

That way, they stayed cool in summer and warm in winter. The tops of the houses were above ground. They were made of wood, brush, and **adobe**.

The Basketmakers farmed on the mesa. This was a change for the people. Before, they had hunted and gathered for food.

Around 750, communities in Mesa Verde grew. Ancestral Puebloans built sandstone houses above ground. The houses were built in

 The Basketmakers grew squash, beans, and corn.

long rows. Some of the houses
had more than one level. Many had
kivas, or pit rooms, dug in front.
Kivas were used for **ceremonies**.

Around 1150, Ancestral Puebloans moved down from the mesa top. They built large **dwellings** in the cliffs. Soon, more than 20,000 people lived in Mesa Verde. But by 1300, everyone was gone. They had all moved south.

No one knows why the Ancestral Puebloans left. Some experts think

Did You Know?

Ancestral Puebloans climbed ladders to move between cliff dwellings.

 The dwellings at Mesa Verde lay untouched for hundreds of years.

their farming failed. Other experts think there was fighting between groups. Either way, the Ancestral Puebloans did not return. But their homes remained.

Chapter 3

A Sacred Site

Today, more than 60,000 Pueblo people live in New Mexico, Arizona, and Texas. They have a special relationship with Mesa Verde. Without their ancestors, the cliff dwellings would not exist.

 Pueblo people wear traditional clothing during a parade.

Many Pueblo people make **pilgrimages** to Mesa Verde. They visit the homes of their ancestors. For them, Mesa Verde is a **sacred** place.

Pueblo people carry an oral history of Mesa Verde. Their ancestors told stories about their lives. Over time, these stories were passed down. They help historians learn about the past.

Historians also learn about Mesa Verde through **archaeology**.

 An archaeologist works in one of the structures at Mesa Verde.

Experts dig to find items that were left behind. These items are called artifacts. Mesa Verde is one of the largest archaeological sites in the United States.

Mesa Verde's artifacts include dwellings, tools, and pottery. They offer clues about how Ancestral Puebloans lived. For example, the dwellings show that they were skilled builders. They used math to design buildings. The pottery shows that they were artists, too. Most

Did You Know?

In 1891, a visitor stole 600 artifacts from Mesa Verde. In 2019, a museum agreed to return some of them to Pueblo peoples.

 Ancestral Puebloan pottery includes complex designs.

likely, Ancestral Puebloans were not struggling to survive. They had time to create art.

Cliff Palace

Cliff Palace was the largest dwelling in Mesa Verde. It had 150 rooms and 23 kivas. Up to 120 people lived inside. Historians believe the site was a social center. It was used for ceremonies and gatherings.

Building Cliff Palace was no easy task. Ancestral Puebloans shaped each sandstone block. They used stones as tools. Next, they mixed soil, water, and ash. This mixture held the blocks together. Last, they added tiny stones to the mixture. This step made the mixture stronger.

Much of Cliff Palace has survived for more than 700 years.

Chapter 4

Visiting Mesa Verde

Thousands of people visit Mesa Verde each year. They come from around the world. There is plenty for visitors to do. For example, they can take a tour with a park ranger. They can explore cliff dwellings.

 People must climb ladders to visit certain parts of Mesa Verde.

These include Cliff Palace, Long House, and Balcony House.

Long House is the second-largest dwelling. Visitors can see a seep spring inside. Rain seeps through the stone of the dwelling. Then it forms a small pool on the floor. Ancestral Puebloans collected water at this spot. They drank it and used it to cook.

Visiting Balcony House is an adventure. Visitors climb ladders up the cliff. Then they squeeze through

Spruce Tree House is one of Mesa Verde's best-preserved dwellings.

a small tunnel. They crawl on their hands and knees. Last, they climb 60 feet (18 m) of uneven steps. Visitors must be careful not to fall.

 Ancestral Puebloans carved artwork onto the walls of the cliffs.

Tours show off the rock art across Mesa Verde. Ancestral Puebloans had no written language. Instead, they told stories through pictures. They carved beautiful stories into their walls. That way, the tales could be shared with future **generations**.

After a tour, visitors can hike trails or visit the park museum. They can watch dances by Pueblo people. They can also camp nearby. They imagine what life was like for Ancestral Puebloans.

Did You Know?

Mesa Verde became a national park in 1906. In its first year, there were 27 visitors.

FOCUS ON
Mesa Verde

Write your answers on a separate piece of paper.

1. Write a letter to a friend describing what you learned about archaeology at Mesa Verde.

2. Which cliff dwelling would you want to see at Mesa Verde? Why?

3. How many Ancestral Puebloans lived in Mesa Verde?
   A. 27
   B. 750
   C. 20,000

4. What is the most likely reason that the Ancestral Puebloans left Mesa Verde?
   A. They didn't have enough food.
   B. They didn't have enough shelter.
   C. They didn't have enough pottery.

5. What does **oral** mean in this book?

*Pueblo people carry an **oral** history of Mesa Verde. Their ancestors told stories about their lives.*

> **A.** written on paper
> **B.** spoken aloud
> **C.** kept a secret

6. What does **uneven** mean in this book?

*Last, they climb 60 feet (18 m) of **uneven** steps. Visitors must be careful not to fall.*

> **A.** strong
> **B.** beautiful
> **C.** rough

Answer key on page 32.

Glossary

adobe
A mixture of mud and straw that is dried and hardened in the sun.

Ancestral Puebloans
People who lived in the American Southwest from approximately 100 CE to 1600 CE.

archaeology
The study of the ancient past, often by digging up buildings or objects from long ago.

ceremonies
Events or actions that are done in a certain way, often for religious reasons.

dwellings
Places where people live.

generations
Groups of people born around the same time.

pilgrimages
Long journeys made for religious reasons.

ruins
Broken pieces of buildings, especially ones from very long ago.

sacred
Having spiritual or religious meaning.

To Learn More

BOOKS

Lajiness, Katie. *Pueblo*. Minneapolis: Abdo Publishing, 2017.

Perdew, Laura. *Colorado*. Minneapolis: Abdo Publishing, 2023.

Thomas, Rachael L. *Uncovering Ancient Artifacts*. Minneapolis: Abdo Publishing, 2019.

NOTE TO EDUCATORS

Visit **www.focusreaders.com** to find lesson plans, activities, links, and other resources related to this title.

Index

A
adobe, 10
Ancestral Puebloans, 6–7, 9–13, 18–20, 24, 26–27
archaeology, 16–17
artwork, 18–19, 26–27

B
Balcony House, 24–25
Basketmakers, 9–10

C
ceremonies, 11, 20
Cliff Palace, 20, 24

F
farming, 10, 13

K
kivas, 11, 20

L
ladders, 12, 24

M
museum, 27

O
oral history, 16

P
pilgrimages, 16
Pueblo people, 15–16, 18, 27

S
sandstone, 10, 20

T
tours, 23–27